LIQUID EDUCATION

Coffee

from bean to
the perfect brew

JASON SCHELTUS

Smith
Street
Books

CONTENTS

Introduction 7

Part One: The Bean 9

Varieties & History 10
Coffee Growing Regions 14
Coffee Production 16
Processing 21
Roasting 27
Freshness 36

Part Two: The Brew 39

Selecting Coffee 40
What to Look For on the Bag 44
Types of Coffee 52
Regional Characteristics 55
Milk & Water 63
Extraction & Brewing 68
Grinding & Equipment 71
Pressured Brewing 81
Non-Pressurised Brewing 89
Coffee Drinks 97

Index 108
About the Author 111

INTRODUCTION

I need my coffee. It's a cry you're likely to hear all over the world and it speaks to the personal investment people feel when it comes to their daily cup. Coffee isn't something we imbibe in a bored or unthinking way – it's something most people care about and put thought into: we have our favourite café or home-brew method; that one barista who knows exactly how we like our cappuccino; that one roastery that sources the best Rwandan beans and roasts them to perfection. Considering we consumed about nine billion kilograms (20 billion pounds) of coffee last year, I think it's safe to say we are obsessed!

I'm no different to anyone else in this regard. A job in a Melbourne café in my early twenties piqued my interest in the mechanics of different brewing methods. A position at a prestigious roastery in London kickstarted my obsession with the provenance and quality of beans. And my role as co-founder and director at Market Lane Coffee has made me focus on the importance of knowing and sharing every step of a coffee's story – from planting, processing and the general journey and philosophy of the producer, to the best way to roast and brew a coffee once it has reached its final destination.

This book is an extension of that project. In the following pages I (humbly!) share what years of research and experience have taught me about coffee so far. I explain the history and science of coffee, and offer explanations for the words you find on coffee bags and hear coffee professionals use – terms like 'pulped natural processing' and 'first crack'. I share my tips for selecting good beans for home brewing, and I offer my simple, tried-and-true recipes for each brew method. For café regulars, there are descriptions of the beverages you see on menus, and a look at the different coffee producing countries and the flavour characteristics unique to each region's output.

To choose a career in coffee is to always be learning, even after years in the industry. There's a lot of information and misinformation floating around about coffee, but it doesn't have to be complicated. I hope this book gives you a greater insight into, and understanding of, one of the world's most delicious beverages – and that it makes tomorrow morning's cup feel even more like your own.

PART one

THE BEAN

VARIETIES & HISTORY

Arabica vs. robusta

There are two main species of coffee grown commercially around the world: *Coffea arabica* and *Coffea robusta*. Both of these species are part of the larger group of plants called the *Coffea* genus, part of the Rubiacea family (which also includes ornamental plants such as gardenias). The main difference between arabica and robusta is their native origins, and therefore what they are conditioned to. Many plants develop bitter-tasting alkaloids (such as caffeine) as a kind of natural pesticide. Arabica is originally from higher altitudes and cooler climates, which means far fewer pests and therefore much lower levels of those bitter alkaloids than you'll find in robusta, which thrives in warmer climates.

Arabica   Robusta

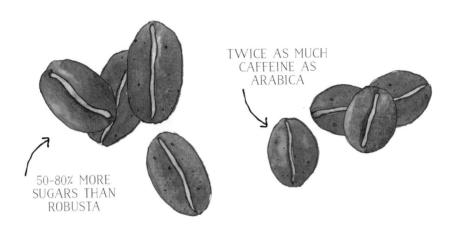

TWICE AS MUCH
CAFFEINE AS
ARABICA

50-80% MORE
SUGARS THAN
ROBUSTA

The characteristics that cause the flavour differences between
arabica and robusta are:

- **Caffeine (alkaloid) content:** robusta has about twice
  as much caffeine as arabica.

- **Sugars:** arabica has 50–80 per cent more sugars
  than robusta.

It's these differences that determine robusta having more rough,
harsh and bitter qualities, while arabica is more sweet and fruity.

History & cultivation

Robusta is grown in many places around the world because of its hardiness, high yield and because it's easy to grow at lower altitudes. It makes up around 40 per cent of the world's coffee exports, with major exporters being Vietnam, Brazil and Indonesia. Despite this, not that much is known about robusta, primarily because it's not grown for quality, and is mainly used for cheaper coffee products, such as instant or pod coffee.

The arabica species is a big family, with many different varieties. Commercially, there are about 150 varieties of arabica grown around the world, but only 30 to 40 that make up most of the world's production. A shrub that prefers to grow in the shade of other trees, or in quite dense forest, *Coffea arabica*'s native habitat is along the edges of the Great Rift Valley, through southern Ethiopia to the eastern parts of South Sudan. Deforestation is a huge threat to native varieties, which is why researchers are collecting and cataloguing thousands of different arabica varieties from native forests such as the Keffa and Yayu forests in the south of Ethiopia, in the interests of genetic preservation and future investment.

In order to select the arabica variety that best suits the growing region, areas should ideally be test-planted with a great number of different varieties, and the best-tasting, most high-yielding variety should be the one chosen for that area. (This method has been applied recently in Rwanda and Kenya, with great results. Scott Laboratories in Kenya selected two varieties that are suited to Kenya's rich volcanic soils, and they produce a very distinctive coffee with blackcurrant and plum flavours.)

However, the reality of how most varieties have ended up where they are has more to do with chance than science. The history of coffee is extremely clouded with myths and stories, but what we do know is that coffee originated in Ethiopia, somehow made its way to the region that is now modern-day Yemen, and was then spread around the world by Dutch and English colonists. It's told that, around the 1850s, a single plant variety called 'typica' was taken from Yemen and spread all over the world, with a few plants eventually mutating into a higher-yielding variety that was called 'bourbon'. It's a neat story, but in all likelihood plants and seeds from many different varieties were taken from Yemen and Ethiopia to places like Brazil and Indonesia between 1820 and 1900.

Old coffee farms in early coffee producing countries like Brazil and Indonesia tend to be planted with what look like one of two 'heirloom varieties' – the first being bourbon, and the second that looks and tastes more like typica. Over generations, these varieties have slowly mutated to adapt to the climates and soils of their new surroundings, meaning an 'original' bourbon variety that has grown in Indonesia for many years is now somewhat different from the same variety growing in Brazil.

Now farmers are able to use these mutations to their advantage, creating new varieties to better suit their needs. A good example is a variety called 'caturra' – which came from a single plant in a field of bourbon that naturally mutated to have shorter nodes on the branches between the leaves and flowers. This shortening of the nodes meant that this particular plant was able to produce more flowers, and therefore more fruit, than a normal bourbon coffee plant. The plant was propagated separately and a new variety was born.

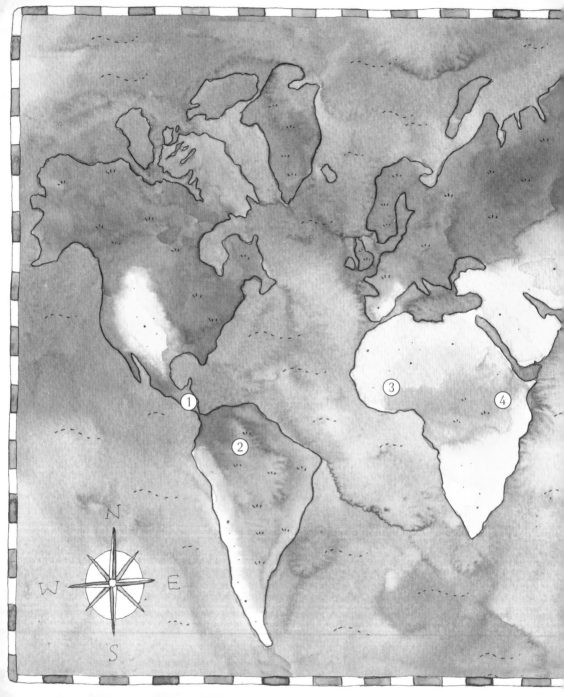

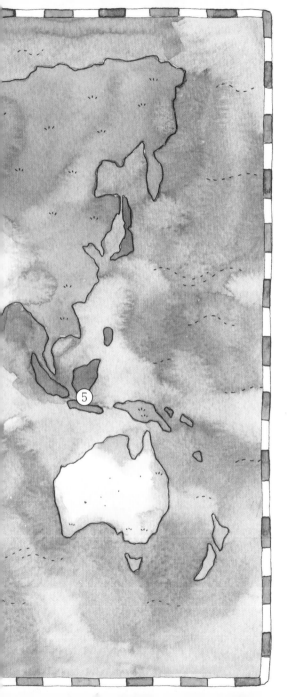

COFFEE GROWING REGIONS

1. CENTRAL AMERICA

2. SOUTH AMERICA

3. WEST AFRICA

4. EAST AFRICA

5. ASIA

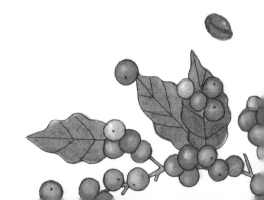

COFFEE PRODUCTION

Coffee growing, harvest practices and processing are extremely different all around the world, mostly due to socio-economic differences, geography, climate and the history of coffee production in each country.

Economic differences

In Brazil, it's common for coffee producers to own thousands of acres of land and produce tens of thousands of bags of coffee each year. These large-scale coffee growers are reasonably wealthy, and often own the infrastructure required to process and export the coffee themselves. For very large farms such as these, the process of growing coffee and harvesting is quite industrialised, with the extensive use of machinery to fertilise, prune and harvest the coffee.

Meanwhile, in countries like Rwanda where individual large-scale landownership is extremely rare, production is completely different. In Rwanda, coffee is grown as a small cash crop for families, in amongst their garden of sustenance crops. The amount grown by these tiny-scale growers is far too small for them to own the infrastructure to process themselves, so they form farmer groups called co-operatives to process and export their coffee in larger lots.

Brazil & Rwanda (to scale)

BRAZIL

RWANDA

These sorts of socio-economic differences make issues surrounding quality assurance, ethical pricing and transparency very complicated, and hence requires the buyer to take different approaches depending on where the coffee has come from.

Ripeness & quality

Throughout the life cycle of coffee, quality can only be preserved, rather than improved or induced. This means that the quality of the coffee you drink at the end of the chain can never be higher than the quality of the cherry that's harvested. Ripeness plays a huge part in quality so it's extremely important that the cherries are picked at the right time.

Even on farms with little or no change in altitude or soil, there is still some variance when it comes to the ideal time to pick each of the cherries, with the amount of ripe cherries on the farm increasing gradually, depending on their age or size. Aside from ripeness, producers also have to consider factors like cost and availability of labour, the physical size of their farm and expected revenue when deciding when to harvest, so one or more of all of these factors tends to be compromised in order for the producer to get the best outcome.

Stages of ripeness

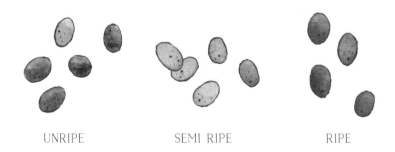

UNRIPE　　　　　　SEMI RIPE　　　　　　RIPE

COFFEE CHERRY
BLOSSOM

COFFEE BEAN

FRUIT PROFILE

The coffee plant

FRUIT
CROSS-SECTION

Picking coffee

Coffee can be harvested (or picked) by machine or by hand. For most places in the world, it is done by hand and it is very slow work. The method and quality of picking can vary enormously. Lower quality producers 'strip pick', whereby all the cherries are stripped off the branch (whether they are ripe or not). Only picking the ripe cherries can improve the flavour of the coffee quite significantly, so a quality-focused producer may direct the pickers to pick only ripe cherries. On a coffee farm that spans a few hundred metres (yards) of altitude, this is particularly important, because the fruit on the lower parts of the farm will ripen well before the fruit on the higher parts of the farm. This small difference of altitude can make a difference of a few days or even a few weeks, so it can have dramatic results when implemented. Of course, this is a slower process and is therefore much more expensive for the producer, so the choice of picking method has to be weighed against the potential price of the coffee.

Lot separation

Sometimes it's only cost-effective for producers to pick part of their crop in this slower way, so smaller 'lots' or 'microlots' are picked with a focus on quality and kept separate from the main harvest so it can be sold for a higher price.

PROCESSING

To store coffee, the seed – or coffee bean – needs to be removed from the fruit and skin. Once it has been removed, it can then be dried for storage and transporting to coffee roasters.

'Processing' refers to the way the coffee bean is removed from its fruit and how it is dried for export. This can be done in a great number of ways, and every country or region has its own method. Traditionally, these methods are determined by how much water is available to the processors at the washing station, and the methods are broken down into these three broad categories: **natural**, **pulped natural** and **washed**.

Natural

The original and simplest method of drying coffee. As the name suggests, after the coffee cherries are harvested from the trees, they are simply laid out to dry in the sun. This method suits producers in places that have very little processing infrastructure, such as Ethiopia and Indonesia, and is the most common way that growers process coffee for their own families. The issue with this method is that it's difficult to control the rate and extent of fermentation due to factors such as ambient temperature and rain. Natural process coffee can taste extremely fruity, or winey, especially as it comes close to over-fermenting.

Washed

The washed method was developed in order to reduce spoilage – common to the natural process method – therefore increasing the value of the coffee for producers. It begins with pulping, which is a mechanical method of removing the skin and some of the fruit. To then remove the small amount of fruit still attached to the seed, the pulped coffee is left in open tanks (sometimes covered with water) for 24–72 hours, during which time the excess flesh is fermented away. The beans are then rinsed and sent out for drying. The fermentation time varies based on climate, as warmer temperatures result in faster fermentation times. The washed method produces a very clean flavour, but quite a mild texture and a lighter body compared to pulped natural or natural.

Pulped natural

The pulped natural process is used quite widely throughout South and Central America, especially in Brazil, where the huge volumes of coffee production means that tank fermentation is not practical. Pulped natural, as it sounds, is right in between the two other methods: the coffee cherry is pulped mechanically and then laid out to dry, with no 'washing' or fermenting step. This method can result in a balance of heavy body with a nice sweetness, and more cleanliness compared to natural process.

While these are the three general categories for processing, every country and region uses endless variations on these methods depending on rainfall, climate and economy.

Drying

Drying is a hugely important part of the coffee production process – it stabilises the beans for shipping, allowing coffee to be sold internationally. Without drying we would not be enjoying coffee from Africa and Central America for long portions of the year. For export, coffee needs to be dried to a maximum moisture content of 12 per cent.

There are many ways for freshly processed coffee to be dried, but they can be broadly categorised into **passive** and **mechanical drying**.

Passive drying

Historically, this is the most popular method of drying coffee. Coffee is laid out to dry in the sun and raked several times a day so that it dries evenly. Passive drying generally takes up to ten days. In regions that have minimal infrastructure, or do not export their coffee, this drying can be done on straw mats, bitumen roads, or simply on the ground. This can lead to quite inconsistent drying and the coffee is easily contaminated with things like stones, sticks or dirt. Larger-scale producers in countries such as El Salvador and Guatemala construct drying patios – large open spaces usually built from concrete – to spread out the coffee to dry on the flat surface. However, patio drying still poses the same contamination problems and it takes up a huge amount of space (on a 25 m²/270 ft² patio, it's possible to dry about 180 kg/395 lb of coffee at a time).

For export, producers work hard to increase the quality of their coffee so they can get a better price. Recently, producers have found that drying the coffee on drying tables that are raised off the ground has increased the airflow around the coffee, leading to more even drying and less spoilage or over-fermentation in the coffee. Even better results have come from stacking these tables into a type of shelving system and housing the drying units in a greenhouse with an openable roof and sides, allowing the producer to control the climate inside the greenhouse to their preferred drying temperature. This method also has great benefits in reducing contamination and conserving space.

RAISED BED METHOD

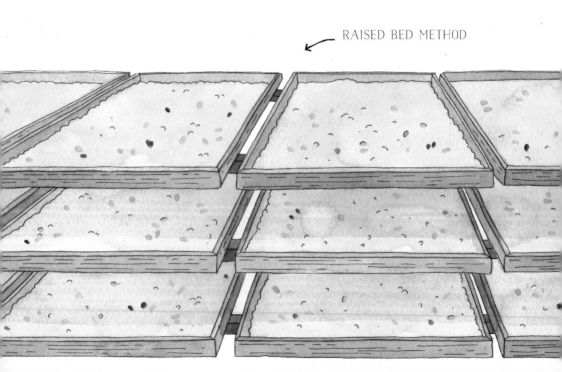

Mechanical drying

Mechanical drying is done when there is a lack of space to dry the coffee, or when vast quantities of production means that the coffee needs to be dried quickly. Mechanical dryers (or *secadora de café*) are usually large drums with perforated walls, which can be as big as 4 m (13 ft) in diameter and 20 m (65 ft) long. The drums turn, agitating the freshly pulped coffee as hot air is blown through.

Mechanical drying has to be done carefully, and monitored constantly, as there is a risk of over-drying, drying too quickly or browning – any of which can be disastrous as they will likely ruin hundreds of kilos (or pounds) of coffee. The air temperature needs to be kept quite low (around 40°C/100°F) and the airflow quite high, so the heat is distributed evenly. Drying at this temperature takes around 24 hours per batch and the heat source is generally a furnace powered by off-cuts from shade and coffee trees, forced through the dryer by a fan.

Not every mill will have mechanical dryers, but they are in a variety of different countries including Brazil, Bolivia and Guatemala. Since they are a large piece of infrastructure, they are limited to countries that can afford to run and maintain such large machines.

In general, mechanical drying results in an inferior flavour compared with passive drying. Therefore, it's common for mechanical dryers to be used in combination with passive drying, especially in places where it can take a long time to achieve the exportable minimum moisture content. For example a mill might dry coffee out on patios for five days down to a moisture of 20 per cent, and then finish the drying off in a mechanical dryer to achieve an even 12 per cent moisture.

ROASTING

Roasting coffee is a kind of alchemy which turns the simple seed of a small fruit into something that can be brewed into an extremely delicious and invigorating drink. The basic premise of roasting is to enable the conditions for grinding and brewing of the coffee seed, and also to brown the bean in order to increase the flavour.

Roasting machines

Since the first roasting machines were patented, there have been two distinct types of machine: **factory roasters** and **shop roasters**. As they sound, the factory roaster was a large machine operated by technicians (historically in quite poor conditions) built to service many retail shops or cafés. They were located in the industrial parts of towns and were not often seen by the public. In fact, they are still so uncommon that it is rare for a person who consumes coffee daily to have seen an unroasted coffee bean.

Shop roasters were designed to be more compact and visually appealing, with a lower overall production capacity, but able to be operated in smaller spaces and in view of the public. These days, there is still a very clear distinction between shop roasters and factory roasters, in their design, appearance and use. The technology surrounding roasting has changed very little since the early 1900s. In fact, with the exception of huge coffee roasting plants, all roasters work from a simple design: coffee is agitated in a cylindrical drum while being heated by hot air and/or a direct flame.

THE SHOP COFFEE ROASTER

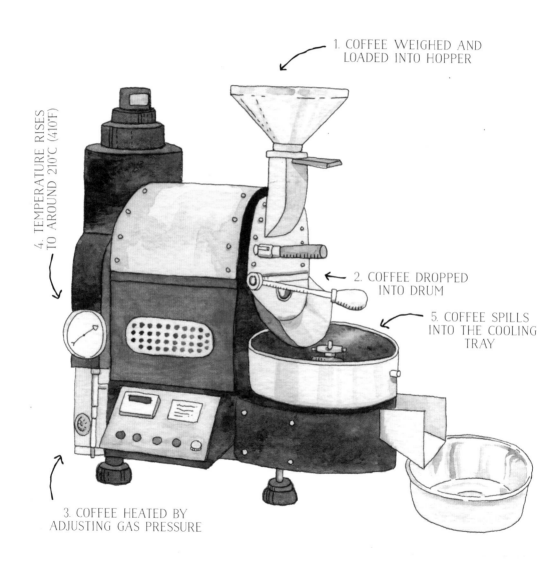

1. COFFEE WEIGHED AND LOADED INTO HOPPER

4. TEMPERATURE RISES TO AROUND 210°C (410°F)

2. COFFEE DROPPED INTO DRUM

5. COFFEE SPILLS INTO THE COOLING TRAY

3. COFFEE HEATED BY ADJUSTING GAS PRESSURE

The roasting process

For a **shop roaster**, the process itself is quite simple:

- Coffee is weighed out, and loaded into the hopper.

- Once the roaster has been preheated to a set temperature, the coffee is dropped into the drum.

- The coffee is heated by adjusting the gas pressure.

- Within 9–15 minutes, the coffee rises in temperature from room temperature up to around 210°C (410°F).

- When the batch is done, the operator opens the door and the coffee spills out into the cooling tray.

- Room temperature air is pulled through the bed of coffee to cool it down, and within 4 minutes, it is ready to be packed.

Factory roasters range from 60 kg (130 lb) batch sizes, up to a few hundred kilo (over 500 lb) batch sizes, and can be capable of roasting tonnes of coffee each day.

Roasting for flavour

There are many factors that influence the flavour that the roasting process creates, these can be summarised as:

Batch size & airflow
The agitation paddles inside a roasting drum are designed and rated for specific amounts of coffee, usually 5, 12, 25 or 60 kg (11, 26, 55 or 130 lb) and much more for factory roasters. Using more coffee than a drum is designed for can result in the coffee roasting unevenly and over too long a period. Using too much coffee can also restrict the amount of air that flows through the drum, again causing it to roast too slowly or not evenly. For example a batch size of 50 per cent of the rated capacity of the drum allows a lot more airflow than a batch size of 100 per cent, so roasters will often use a batch size that is 60–80 per cent of the rated roaster capacity. Batch size also influences the type of heat transfer, with an over-full drum imparting more conductive heat transfer than is required.

Time
For all types of roasters, the overall roasting of the batch will influence the taste. Generally, coffee roasted for under four minutes will not have a well-developed flavour and can taste grassy. And, in general, coffee that is roasted over a period longer than 15 minutes will taste flat and similar to rye bread. Usually, the longer a batch has been roasted, the lower the perceivable acidity in the cup, and the heavier the body will be.

Final temperature

In many ways, the temperature at which the coffee is dropped out of the drum is the most important. Light roasts can taste 'green', vegetal, or malty when roasted too light, and dark roasts can taste harsh, overly bitter, or dry. The best roast degree for a particular coffee is one that highlights the variety and regional characteristics, and does not show any signs of under- or over-roasting.

The temperature profile

The way the coffee reaches its final end temperature and the time this takes has an effect on the taste produced by roasting. This rate of increase is called the 'roast profile'. In general, an ideal roast profile for coffee will have the temperature always increasing, but the rate of increase in temperature continuously decreasing. The temperature profile also encompasses the time between the start of the roast and first crack, and the time between first crack and the end of the roast.

Cooling time

If the coffee is not cooled fast enough, it can keep cooking in the cooling tray, creating a malty or rye-bread flavour in the coffee. Once dropped out of the roaster, coffee needs to be cooled in four minutes or less to avoid these flavours affecting the batch.

Stages of roasting

Coffee goes through some big physical changes during the roasting process and some important chemical changes that increase the flavour potential. It isn't possible to make a coffee brew out of dried, unroasted beans – they need to be dried to an even lower moisture content, and the coffee flavour as we know it is created by a browning process, as described below.

First crack

As heat is applied to the green bean by air or from the drum walls, the moisture is forced away from the heat source, inwards towards the centre of the bean. As this happens, the outer edges of the bean start to become more brittle as they dry, and some light browning of the coffee starts to occur when the outside temperature reaches around 160°C (320°F). This drying of the outer layers of the bean creates a temperature difference between the surface of the bean and the moisture front. During this period, between 160°C and 180°C (320°F and 350°F), the pressure inside the bean increases until the point at which it fractures open slightly, releasing energy in the form of sound and heat. As the coffee approaches this point, called 'first crack', the heat applied to the coffee bean is lowered, so that the rate of temperature increase slows down so as not to scorch the coffee. On the other hand, if this pressure increase takes too long, the cells do not expand enough during first crack, causing the coffee to brown unevenly.

THE ROASTING BEAN

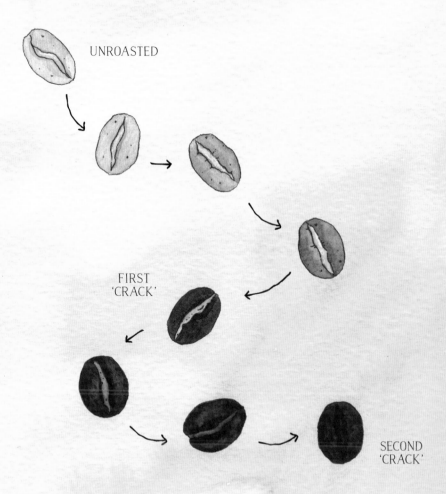

UNROASTED

FIRST
'CRACK'

SECOND
'CRACK'

Browning

The browning stage consists of eight different processes or degradations, but the main two are caramelisation and the Maillard reaction. Caramelisation begins around 160°C (320°F) but on its own, does not influence the flavour of the coffee a great deal. Most of this work is done by the Maillard reaction, which occurs between 160°C (320°F) and the end point of the roast. The Maillard reaction occurs between amino acids and sugars when heat is applied, browning the coffee and producing over 800 different aromatic compounds, resulting in the complex aromas we associate with coffee.

The challenge when it comes to roasting is that every coffee bean is different – whether it's from a different country or altitude or coffee variety – each type will require a slightly different roast profile to produce the best flavour.

The perfect roast?

How can we tell if coffee is roasted well or not? It's a hard question to answer, because everyone has their own idea of what coffee should taste like, and different roasters have different priorities and preferences for taste. The short answer is to taste that particular batch to find out whether it's been done well, in a careful way that is the same across different batches. The long answer is that there are many styles of roasting around the world – from 'wood-fired' to Nordic-style and Italian espresso – and many of these profiles are sympathetic to the local culture, cuisine, water and style of coffee making. So, while a particular roast may not be that palatable to you, it may still be exactly what the roasting company was after.

Coffee from each farm changes year to year, similar to the way that wine from the same vineyard does, and so different years can produce very different flavours. These changes are caused by differing yields, fertilising, pruning and, of course, weather differences. This means that a roasting profile that worked for one particular coffee in one year may not work as well for the same coffee in a different year. It is hard to predict what these changes in flavour profile might mean for a roasting profile, and it simply means that for each coffee, it will need to be adjusted from season to season. Green coffee will also change after it has been harvested and processed, and therefore it is important to continually taste various roasting profiles for each coffee throughout the profile's duration.

In my opinion, coffee is roasted well when you can taste its regional and cultivar characteristics, and the taste is sweet, balanced and clean. I hope that this is a common goal among roasters, and something that customers would look for, but unfortunately, currently there is not a great deal of discussion about roasting styles, goals, or differences. The more these things are talked about, the easier it is for consumers to articulate their preferences.

FRESHNESS

One of the big reasons coffee is imported in its unroasted form is that roasted coffee changes and stales quickly. Unroasted coffee remains in a stable condition for many months after it has been processed and dried – up to 18 months in some cases (but 12 months is more common). Whereas roasted coffee can stale in a matter of weeks, and much more quickly if not stored well.

The actual process roasted coffee goes through when it stales is quite complex and not well-understood enough to stop it from happening. But simply, there is a degradation of acids that are created during the roasting process, causing the coffee to lose its vibrancy and slowly develop an unpleasant sourness. During the roasting process, a large amount of carbon dioxide (CO_2) is formed in the coffee as a result of the caramelisation process. As the coffee ages, the CO_2 diffuses out of the coffee bean over a period of a few weeks. During this process, the coffee oxidises and then the flavour slowly degrades over the following few months.

This ageing process is sped up by exposure to light, heat and oxygen, so limiting the coffee's exposure to these is very important. Most coffee roasters now store their freshly roasted coffee in foil-lined bags, preventing exposure to light and oxygen.

It's common for people to ask, 'What's the best way to store coffee?', and it's a difficult question because the assumption is that if you store it well enough it will last for a long time, and unfortunately, this just isn't the case. No matter how well coffee is stored, it will oxidise and the flavour will degrade. I recommend buying small amounts of coffee frequently, storing it in a cool dark place, like your pantry, and using it within a few weeks.

PART two

THE BREW

SELECTING COFFEE

Choosing coffee for home can be difficult and sometimes intimidating. As with wine, there can be a lot of technical and marketing terms used that often aren't very clear. Hopefully I can shed some light on what information matters the most when selecting coffee, and what information you can chalk up to marketing. There are a couple of certifications to look out for, but generally the industry doesn't have any fixed standards as to what should be printed on the bags for customers.

The importance of traceability

Until very recently, coffee was traded as a commodity. There were many different grades for different origins, based on quality, altitude and even the physical size of the coffee bean. For a young industry, trading in this way makes sense, after all, how many roasters and customers could the world sustain? Well, very many as it turns out. Improving coffee's traceability started out because roasters wanted better quality lots of coffee for their customers and more consistent quality year to year. Coffee brokers and roasters started to look for individual or groups of farmers who were interested in making improvements to their processes in exchange for a higher price. These improvements were often as simple as only picking ripe cherries, or only selecting lots for export from the highest parts of a farm. But the consequences are significant – changing coffee from a commodity to a traceable, quality product means huge improvements for consumers and better prices for coffee producers.

So how traceable does it have to be to make a difference? This is a very difficult question to answer, because each coffee producing country has a different socio-economic background, and therefore a unique economic relationship between coffee producer, coffee exporter and roaster. Poorer countries tend to have more government structure surrounding the export and trade of coffee, whereas more developed countries tend to have fewer mediating bodies.

In countries such as Ethiopia, Kenya and Rwanda, coffee co-operatives can be made up of thousands of members, each being a small family with only a few coffee trees to tend to and look after (one coffee tree can produce a few kilos/pounds of coffee per season). In circumstances such as these, traceability is generally limited to the larger co-operative name and the region in which the co-operative is based. In more developed countries such as Brazil, Guatemala or Costa Rica, vast coffee plantations can be owned by a single person or a single family, meaning traceability is far more precise.

To make a difference to the lives of the producers, traceability needs to extend down to a washing station level, and ideally further to a smaller group. Defining larger groups of people such as whole regions means that there is very little benefit to identification.

Making informed choices

As with many products, knowing the source of the coffee can help to inform consumers about other issues they might care about. Having the ability to speak directly with coffee producers allows good roasters and retailers to gain insight into that producer's practices, which not only helps in quality assurance but also allows for transparency on two main ethical issues linked to coffee production: **environmental concerns** and **child labour**.

Environmental concerns

The negative environmental impacts of coffee production can include waterway contamination, clear-felling of forests, and the development of monocultures. The use of fertilisers is common in Central and South America (although less so in Africa), and overuse or careless application can lead to acidification of soil and waterways, killing native wildlife and biodiversity. All water runoff from coffee processing needs to be treated to kill any remaining bacteria or sugars so as not to change the chemistry of the waterways in areas surrounding production.

The ethical implications of destroying local environments to boost crops are very serious – many communities rely on a healthy environment to produce subsistence crops, especially in the poorest parts of the world.

Child labour

Child labour is a grave concern for the coffee industry. It's an extremely complicated issue, and one that doesn't have a simple solution or rule that can be applied to avoid it. It's tragic that it still occurs in coffee producing countries, and it requires efforts from all parts of the industry to ensure it comes to an end.

Without traceability, these concerns can go unchecked and uninhibited. With traceability, consumers can be empowered to make informed decisions about what products and producers to support. As regulation in the coffee industry is not yet tight enough to prevent these concerns, consumers have a responsibility to try and make a difference with the choices that we make.

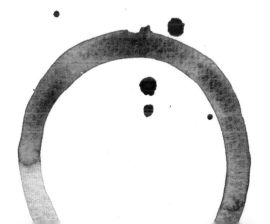

WHAT TO LOOK FOR ON THE BAG

A few things to look for when buying coffee beans.

HARVEST INFORMATION

ROAST DATE

ESPRESSO
R O A S T

HULIA, COLOMBIA
·····················
PROCESS WASHED
·····················
ALTITUDE 1600-1700
·····················
ROASTED 2/4/15

TYPE OF ROAST

CERTIFICATIONS

Roast date

Good coffee retailers or roasters should only sell coffee for a short period after it has been roasted, so that you can enjoy it while it is fresh. Well-roasted coffee doesn't have to be consumed immediately for it to be at its best, but it should be consumed within 4–6 weeks of roasting. If you're buying coffee from a trusted retailer or roaster, and you know that they're careful about their stock age and rotation, then you obviously don't need to check the coffee is fresh every time you make a purchase. But, if you're trying coffee from a new roaster, I would recommend checking that the coffee has been roasted within the last week. If there is no obvious roast date on the bag, it may be linked to a batch number that a staff member can help you with. If there is clearly no roast date on the bag, it is safe to assume it was roasted months ago, and therefore stale. See Freshness on page 36 for more on roasted coffee age.

Harvest information

In most cases, coffee is only harvested once or twice a year. The harvest cycle for coffee is based on a flowering cycle and rain, so it's different in every country and even in different regions of the same country. The altitude that the coffee is grown at will also affect the cycle, with higher altitude grown coffees flowering at a more consistent time of year than lower altitude grown coffee. It is made further complicated by large coffee estates that have a wide altitude range; coffee growing at the lower parts of the farm will be ready first, and coffee growing at higher parts of the farm will be harvested later. As you can see, it's complicated.

The green coffee itself will taste best when roasted and consumed within 12–18 months of harvest. A good retailer or roaster will only sell coffee that has been harvested within this time, but again, if you're buying from a retailer or roaster you don't know, the best thing to do is to ask whether it is current crop or fresh crop, and hopefully they can provide this information. The issue for roasters is that it's difficult to always maintain fresh crop coffee, because purchasing one year's worth of coffee from one particular country means that it has to last a whole year. Fresh crop or current crop is any coffee that has been harvested in the last 12–18 months.

Certifications

There are a few certifications available to coffee producers, for the benefit of the retail customer. The most common certifications are certified organic, fair trade, Rainforest Alliance and Cup of Excellence.

Certified organic Internationally, there are many different associations that can administer organic certification, and different food labelling laws apply too. If you want to support organic farming practices, it's worth noting that organic farming can exist without certification, but it's not all that common. Bolivia is a notable exception – their coffee industry is very small, and most of the producers have a special relationship with the environment, caring for it as if it were a whole living entity. Ethiopia is also notable, where a lot of the coffee is grown by individuals, a few plants at a time.

Australia has particularly lax labelling laws when it comes to foods. Essentially, you can label anything as 'organic' even if it is literally dripping with fungicides and pesticides. If a food is labelled 'certified organic', then it does have to conform to strict rules applied by a few associations, so always look out for a particular certification rather than just the word 'organic'.

FAIRTRADE

Fair trade

Fair trade guarantees a minimum price paid to coffee farmers. It's currently USD$1.40 per pound for washed arabica coffee. This price is less than half the price that is paid for high quality coffee, as you would find in good coffee shops around the world, and about 25 cents per pound more than the current 'C' price for washed arabica coffee (a floating futures trading commodity price).

The fair trade price is a guaranteed minimum for co-operatives that qualify, but the certification does not assure buyers of any minimum quality standards other than washed arabica. Choosing fair trade certified coffee over similar lower quality coffees, or commodity traded coffees can be a good choice to ensure a better price is paid to producers, but if you are buying high quality coffee then the price paid to the producer will be based on the quality rather than the commodity or fair trade price.

Cup of Excellence

Cup of Excellence is a national coffee quality competition, held in a number of different coffee producing countries each year. It is free for producers to enter, and they are only required to submit a small sample of their coffee. The competition is independently audited to ensure it is free from influence or corruption, and ensures buyers have confidence in the system. The best 30–40 coffees of that country for that year are determined initially by a national jury, and then finally by an international jury representative of international buyers. Once the final coffees have been ranked, the top coffees (scoring 85/100 or over) are awarded Cup of Excellence, and then sold at auction over the internet. The starting price for these coffees is USD$5 per pound, and the auction drives the price up from that, usually to USD$8–15 per pound, but it has gone as high as USD$45 per pound in the past.

The aim of the competition is to connect coffee producers with coffee roasters or brokers who have a common goal of high quality. The competition helps to build relationships between growers and roasters, while establishing and quantifying the value and quality of their coffee. This means that in years to come, whether the coffee is submitted to the competition or not, the producer can sell their coffee at a premium price based on its quality. If a bag of coffee has a Cup of Excellence sticker on it, you can be assured the quality has been checked many, many times, and a great price was paid to the producer.

Type of roast

Roast degree is referred to quite a lot on bags of coffee, using words like 'strong' or 'deep' roast, which, for the most part, don't mean anything. There aren't any standards when it comes to roast degree or colour, and even if there were, they might not tell you enough about the roast to make a meaningful difference to the flavour. Most roasters tend to stick to one style of roasting, and so if you appreciate one of their styles of coffee, then chances are you will enjoy other coffees they offer too.

Broadly, coffee can be roasted to suit espresso-style brewing or filter-style brewing (like plunger or pour over). The difference between them being that espresso roasts are usually roasted to a higher temperature to compensate for the higher acidity and strength that espresso machines draw out of the bean. I would recommend looking for espresso-roasted coffees if you brew with an espresso machine or stovetop percolator at home, and filter-roasted coffees for every other brewing method.

Coffee flavour

There are plenty of descriptive terms used on coffee packaging, but most of them aren't particularly meaningful as the qualities they describe should be a given when it comes to coffee.

Strong

For the most part, when the word 'strong' is used to describe a type of coffee bean, it's used to mean the opposite of insipid. So it's referring to the strength of the flavour, not the strength of the coffee, which is determined by how much coffee you extract in a brew (and not by the type of coffee bean). For whole bean coffee, darker roasts will taste stronger than lighter roasts, but this is a result of the way the coffee shatters when it is ground, not the type of coffee itself.

Other words that fall into this category are: **smooth**, **rich**, **robust**, **bold** and **full-bodied**. If you're buying good quality coffee, all of these should be assumed, so they don't actually tell you anything about the flavour of the coffee.

When looking for flavour indicators on the bag, I usually only refer to the **country of origin**, and the **processing method**. The country of origin will give a broad idea about the flavour of the coffee (see Regional characteristics, pages 55–62) and the processing method will define whether it will taste very clean, such as washed or pulped natural, or whether the flavour will have more complex ferment characteristics coming through, such as natural process coffees.

TYPES OF COFFEE

I always recommend buying coffee beans because they have been through the least amount of processing. There are, of course, other types of coffee products available, but they sacrifice quality for convenience. The two most popular ones are:

Instant coffee Instant coffee, or soluble coffee, is made over a long process in a factory. Basically, raw green coffee is imported, then roasted, then very finely ground. At this point the coffee liquid is extracted from the ground coffee to a very high percentage. The resulting liquid is dehydrated and crystallised, and these crystals are instant coffee granules. So when you make instant coffee you're essentially rehydrating a coffee brew. Instant coffee is much more expensive to manufacture than whole bean coffee, because it takes 300 g (10½ oz) of whole bean coffee to produce 100 g (3½ oz) of instant coffee (the maximum amount of the whole bean coffee you can dissolve is about 30 per cent). To compensate, instant coffee is made with cheaper green coffee, and so the taste is much more harsh than better quality whole bean coffee.

Coffee pods

Exactly how pod coffee is made is a secret carefully guarded by manufacturers, but essentially it's a mix of soluble (instant) coffee and finely ground whole bean coffee in a vacuum-sealed plastic or aluminium pod. The machines used to brew the coffee are usually made specifically for the manufacturer of the particular pods, and are made to brew the coffee with a very particular water pressure and temperature. Usually the coffee is brewed under much higher pressure than regular espresso, which gives the coffee more crema than it would have otherwise. The only benefit of pod coffee is that it's convenient – there is very little to clean up and very little action to take when brewing a coffee. The downsides of pod coffee are:

- the flavour is inferior

- they're environmentally unfriendly

- the pods are expensive

- there's usually very little traceability

- the machines are expensive and usually only work with the one type of coffee provider.

The most pertinent criticism of pod coffee is the environmental impact. The pods are not easily recycled through domestic recycling programs, so it's estimated that each year billions of pods are disposed of in landfill waste.

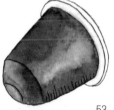

Whole bean or ground?

It's always better to buy whole bean coffee and grind it fresh than to buy pre-ground coffee. In whole bean form, coffee will age slowly, over three or four weeks, but once it's been ground, the ageing process happens much more rapidly. The speed depends on a couple of factors (such as heat, and exposure to light and oxygen), but grind size has the biggest impact. Grinding greatly increases the surface area of the coffee (and the finer the grind, the greater the surface area) which means that the carbon dioxide escapes much more quickly than it would from the whole bean coffee, taking with it some of the volatile aromatics. It's these aromatics that give coffee its unique flavour in the cup, and give it its distinctive regional character.

The increase in surface area also causes the coffee to oxidise at a much faster rate than it would in whole bean form. Oxidisation can cause rancid and sour flavours, masking some of the natural flavour of the coffee. Coffee doesn't really go off per se, but as it goes stale, the natural flavours of the coffee become muted and the oxidised flavours become more dominant.

If you don't have a grinder at home, or you only have a small whirly blade grinder, I would recommend purchasing ground coffee for plunger or French press only, and only drinking espresso from cafés rather than trying to make it at home with pre-ground coffee.

REGIONAL CHARACTERISTICS

There are a number of factors which make each coffee taste different. The four major ones are: variety, processing, growing conditions, and, of course, roasting. Local climate or regional characteristics can be defined by things like altitude and soil type or even rainfall; different growing regions within the same country can produce very different flavours.

For example, coffees grown in the western province of Rwanda tend to be very heavy bodied with a rich sweetness like plum, whereas coffee produced in the southern parts of Rwanda tend to be much lighter bodied, more floral and more delicate. This is despite the coffee being grown at a similar altitude, with the same variety of coffee, and with a similar method of processing. The differences could be attributed to micro-climates and soil types, but it is not clear exactly what causes these differences. Every coffee producing country does have many small micro-climates and regions where coffee is grown, each with their own unique flavour profile.

There are far too many regions to go through in detail, so in this section I will briefly describe regional characteristics from the most common coffee producing countries to give you a broad overview.

Brazil

Brazilian coffee is one of the most popular choices among coffee drinkers. It's usually good value in terms of quality of flavour for dollar amount, attributed to the large volumes of coffee that are grown in Brazil, and the mechanised nature of the production. '.

A lot of the coffee-growing country in Brazil is relatively flat, or at least gently sloping. This terrain is suited to vast, uninterrupted coffee plantations, making mechanised coffee picking an attractive possibility. With large volumes of coffee come economies of scale too, meaning processing coffee for export in Brazil is cheaper than in places such as Central America.

Coffee grown in Brazil is usually quite low in acidity, with a nutty flavour characteristic. Coffee from Bahia in the northeast of Brazil tends to be heavier bodied with more acidity, sometimes with flavours reminiscent of cherry or plum, paired with nutty or chocolate characteristics. When grown at lower altitudes, this coffee tends to have more of a peanut flavour, and can be quite harsh.

Because of its lower price and low-acidity flavour profile, Brazilian coffees have traditionally been a popular base for espresso blends over the years, often balanced with higher-acidity coffees from Central America.

Ethiopia

Ethiopia is one of the world's largest exporters of coffee. All coffee originated in and around Ethiopia, and it remains home to thousands of native varieties, many that are still untasted! The flavour of Ethiopian coffee is very distinctive, and falls into two main categories: washed and natural process. These terms refer to the amount of water used in the processing method (see pages 21–22). Natural process, or unwashed, coffee is predominantly produced in the eastern and northeastern parts of Ethiopia, where the climate is drier; and washed coffees produced in the west, southwest and central areas – from the capital Addis Ababa along the Great Rift Valley to Sudan.

Washed Ethiopian coffees taste very floral, often with flavours like lemon, black tea, orange blossom and nectarine. They can be very perfumey, with intense aromas of rose or butterscotch. Their light characteristics suits them to filter-brewing methods like pour over, plunger or AeroPress.

Natural process Ethiopian coffees are very different from washed, usually much heavier bodied, and often described as 'boozy' – a word used to evoke the very heavy and fruity flavours produced in red wine. Flavours in natural process Ethiopians can be subtle and fruity with blueberry and plum, or more intense with cooked fruit, date and plum, and even bubblegum. Because of their heavy body and intense fruit character, natural process Ethiopian coffees are used on their own as an interesting espresso coffee, or as a small proportion in more conventional espresso blends.

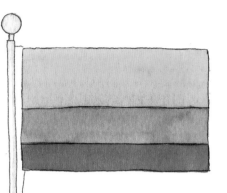

Colombia

Colombia has a huge range of micro-climates and different growing regions, and its range in coffee flavour reflects this. The southern areas of Colombia have traditionally produced high quality coffee, especially from regions such as Nariño and Huila due to their altitude, natural biodiversity, rainfall and proximity to the equator. Coffees from these regions can be medium bodied and floral, with more ripe fruit flavours like plum and blackcurrant. They are usually quite high in acidity and complexity of flavour, making them excellent choices for filter-coffee brewing. Because of the great range in growing regions, Colombian coffees are also often selected for espresso blends.

Colombia has experienced one of the biggest changes in climate due to global warming and El Niño affecting coffee-growing areas. Rainfall has generally increased and become more frequent, meaning that in some places coffee will flower almost all year, and therefore produce fruit year round. This has economic consequences for producers who rely on seasonal labour, and the seasonal labourers themselves. Colombia has also seen an increase in the frequency of warmer nights. At medium altitudes, cold nights are important to kill off funghi and pests, so hospitable temperatures means more damage to coffee plants. Because of the huge amount of rainfall that Colombia receives, all export-grade coffee is washed process.

Guatemala

Guatemala has some beautiful coffee-growing regions – from Antigua, which is surrounded by three giant volcanoes, to the rainforested and biodiverse Cobán. The range of coffee flavours also reflects this geographical diversity, from the heavy-bodied and chocolatey coffees found in Antigua to the rich and fruity coffees found in the highlands of Huehuetenango.

Coffee in Guatemala is almost entirely grown under shade. In some cases, like Antigua, to protect against frost. In densely forested regions such as Cobán and Huehuetenango, a huge variety of trees are used as shade, including inga and macadamia trees, fruit trees, and gravileas. Encouraging natural diversity in shade trees helps keep the environment healthy, promoting wildlife and robust soil.

Because of its range in flavour, Guatemalan coffee can be really well suited to espresso in blends or by itself, and other Guatemalan coffees are really well suited to filter-coffee brewing methods.

Rwanda

Over the last 20 years, Rwanda's story has been one of healing and recovery from the devastating genocide of its past. Coffee has played a huge part in rebuilding Rwanda's economy and society, having been identified as a cash crop with huge potential for quality and profit for export. Several international aid agencies have worked with Rwandans to build washing stations, collection points, schools and infrastructure to help improve quality and quantity of exportable coffee. Rwanda is now producing some of the most interesting and sweetest coffees in the world.

Rwanda is affectionately called the 'Land of a Thousand Hills', and, after seeing the beautiful landscape you will understand why. It is luminous with vibrant plant life and colourful local fabrics. Rwanda's geography and climate are extremely well suited to coffee growing, with high altitude, proximity to the equator and an enormous amount of rainfall. Coffee in Rwanda is grown by individuals and families with just a few trees as cash crops. The coffee cherries they produce are sold to washing stations, or larger farmer groups who then process the coffee for export. Drinking coffee is not really part of the culture in Rwanda, so everything is exported.

A great deal of Rwanda's coffee growing occurs in the northwest near the huge Lake Kivu. Coffee grown in this region tends to be very sweet and rich, with flavours like raisin and plum, which are great for espresso. In the south of Rwanda, the coffees tend to be much more floral and lighter bodied, so are suited to filter-coffee brewing.

Indonesia

Coffee was first brought to Indonesia by the Dutch. The first coffee planted in Indonesia was arabica typica, most likely introduced in the late 1600s or early 1700s via one of the other Dutch colonies such as India. Most of the early varieties of coffee planted in Indonesia were wiped out in the late 1800s by coffee leaf rust, a fungus that also wiped out all of the coffee plantations in Sri Lanka. Most of the typica was replanted with robusta, as it's a much hardier plant and much less susceptible to coffee leaf rust.

Nowadays coffee from Indonesia is categorised by growing region, such as Java, Sumatra, Sulawesi and Bali. Unlike any other coffee producing country, the flavour of Indonesian coffee is predominantly influenced by the unique processing method called 'wet hulling'. The process itself is very similar to washed processing of coffee, but the coffee will remain pulped but not dried for much longer, often for days, giving the coffee a flavour like wet tobacco, earth or sometimes ferment.

Indonesia is also home to the controversial civet cat coffee, called kopi luwak,. The story that people like to tell about this coffee is highly questionable: that wild cats forage only the ripest fruit from coffee trees which are then collected by farmers once it has passed through the cat's digestive system. Several recent investigations into how kopi luwak is produced has shown that the vast majority is produced by employing the cruel practice of force-feeding caged animals. As such, I would recommend avoiding kopi luwak entirely.

Kenya

Kenyan coffee is famous around the world, and for good reason. Kenya has produced distinctive coffees with vibrant acidity for many years, and has commanded a high price accordingly. A lot of the best coffee in Kenya is grown between Nairobi and Mount Kenya, from small regions including Nyeri and Thika. Kenya has an advanced centralised auction system to help farmer groups get good prices for their coffee. Unlike Rwanda, there is a local market for roasted coffee and its consumption – especially in Nairobi, which attracts wealthier individuals from many African nations.

Kenyan coffee growers have worked hard to develop the best combination of coffee varieties for their rich volcanic soil. The government has selected a couple of varieties that they believe produce the best flavour: SL28 and SL34 as well as a new variety called Ruiru 11 which is more disease- and pest-resistant but is somewhat inferior in flavour. It's hoped that with more research and testing, Kenya will improve its yield and production, as well as reduce the need for synthetic fertilisers and fungicides, through variety selection. This research has also benefitted producers in other countries, with El Salvador trialling the SL28 variety with some success.

The flavour profile of Kenyan coffee is very distinct – it has ripe blackcurrant flavours with very high acidity and medium body. The coffees are normally described as being very juicy, reminiscent of ripe fruit. With good roasting they can be very delicate, floral and sweet, suitable for espresso and filter-coffee brewing.

MILK & WATER

How water affects flavour

Water plays a very important part in coffee brewing, not only through its chemistry and its ability to extract coffee, but also as an ingredient. Water can make up 98.7 per cent of the brew for filter coffee by weight, and about 90 per cent of black espresso coffee, so any flavour taints or problems with the water will carry through to the brewed coffee. Common taints include chlorine, sulphur or metallic flavours from old pipes. It's extremely important to remove any taints before using water to brew coffee, which can be done easily with a simple carbon filter.

Ideal water chemistry for brewing coffee can be a very complicated matter, and one that very few people (myself included) understand fully. Research has found that to achieve the best taste when brewing coffee there is certainly an ideal mineral composition, pH level and so on in water, but the challenge is that the composition of water is different everywhere. You'll find differences in the water within parts of a city, let alone country- and world-wide. For the most part, cafés and roasters use a simple carbon filter on their water supply to remove flavour taints and then adjust their roasting to deal with any specific properties of the water supply. So, unless you have a lot of spare time on your hands or you're a chemical engineer, I would recommend using a simple carbon water filter, and talking to your local roaster about water.

FULL FAT milk

1 LT

WHOLE MILK

BIO DYNAMIC

FARMER GILL'S Milk ORGANIC

Choosing the right milk

Since the early 1900s, milk production has slowly become more and more industrialised. Milk from large dairies is highly processed – from splitting fat content down to tenths of a single per cent and reconstituting it, to homogenisation processes which alter protein structures and make digestion difficult.

If you can buy milk from a farmers' market or directly from a producer, I would recommend doing so. Small-scale dairy farms tend to produce better quality milk than larger-scale operations. And ideally, look for certified organic milk, preferably biodynamic, which ensures the soil and environment are closely considered when farming dairy. In most western countries, milk sold through supermarkets for consumption is legally required to be pasteurised by heat treatment. The most common method is to heat the milk to a high temperature (around 96°C/205°F) for a very short time, which is known as flash pasteurisation. A more gentle method is to heat the milk to a lower temperature (around 65°C/149°F) over a longer time. This method is less harsh on the milk, and seems to retain a better flavour than flash pasteurisation.

Good pasture, breed and processing are the main factors that positively impact the flavour of milk. Cows should be fed a good variety of grasses and flowers, however, in much of the dairy industry cows are fed just one or two varieties of grain, which produces a very simple and bland milk. Holstein-Friesian are the world's most popular dairy cow due to their capacity for high milk production, but Jersey cattle are still fairly common and produce a superior-flavoured milk.

Tips on texturising milk

Heating milk for espresso drinks using steam has many benefits, the primary ones being that it's very fast, sometimes only taking 15 seconds to heat; and the swirling action of the milk changes the texture of the milk as it warms it, making it thicker and more voluminous, resulting in a rich and creamy mouthfeel.

The best temperature for milk is 63–65°C (145–149°F) – hot enough that you can't gulp it down, but a perfect sipping temperature.

There are a couple of tricks to making silky textured milk for your cappuccino or caffè latte that will have you steaming like an expert in no time.

- Always start with fresh milk and a clean milk pitcher. Once milk has been heated and textured, the proteins are structally different from those of cold milk, and can't be returned to the prior state by chilling the milk again. Texturing previously heated milk will give you a drier, more bubbly result.

- Fill the milk pitcher to about two-thirds full. This gives you the ideal amount for good agitation, without running the risk of milk spilling over the sides of the pitcher.

- Add air to the milk before it gets hot. Using the steam wand, gently break the surface of the milk in the pitcher to incorportate some air, but only until the milk is warm. Once the milk is above 50°C (122°F) it doesn't incorporate air as well as it does when it is cold – it tends to make the milk more bubbly rather than stretched.

- Agitate. I find the best textured milk is created when there is a lot of movement of milk in the pitcher. I aim to create a whirlpool of spinning milk as soon as I start steaming. This agitation creates a similar effect to whipping egg whites, making the milk thicker and beautifully textured.

The end result should be milk that is very glossy in appearance, and when you swirl the pitcher the milk should be slightly thickened, with a consistency similar to pouring cream.

EXTRACTION & BREWING

Brewing coffee can be fun and easy, but a lot of people still find it daunting. I think much of this apprehension is because it's not very common to see coffee brewed, or if it is, it is done behind expensive machinery. A big barrier for people to get into brewing their own coffee is the equipment needed to get started, but there are many ways to brew coffee, and some of them do not require expensive equipment. At its most basic, coffee is brewed with hot water, and then the grounds are separated from the mixture with a filter or gravity.

About extraction & strength

Only a portion of coffee is soluble in water. The most you can dissolve in water is 30 per cent of the weight of ground coffee, but to get the best flavour and balance, around 20 per cent is ideal. A few things contribute to the rate at which solubles are extracted from coffee, and they are:

- **water temperature**: a higher temperature will extract more

- **particle size**: a smaller particle size will allow more extraction

- **agitation**: the more the coffee is agitated, the greater the extraction, think of jiggling a tea bag

- **pressure**: the pressure under which water is forced through a bed of coffee will impact the level of extraction.

The variable that has the biggest influence, and the one we change most often, is the particle size, or what we call grind size. This is adjusted on grinders by changing the distance between the two burr sets – the closer the burrs are together, the finer the grind.

The size of coffee particles is very hard to communicate because it's so hard to measure. So we can relate it to other substances that we are familiar with – the particle size for plunger-ground coffee is close to the coarseness of rough sand and at the other end of the spectrum the particle size for espresso-ground coffee is between table salt and a fine powder. The best way to get started is to ask for an example of grind size from your local roaster, this way you can feel the right size between your fingers and understand the range.

As discussed on page 51, the word 'strong' is generally used in coffee marketing to mean 'flavourful'. In reality, the strength of a coffee is a measure of the heaviness of the texture of the brew. Or, to put it another way, strength is the weight of the mouthfeel of the coffee.

Strength can be measured by calculating the dissolved solids that are held in the brew, and these solids can make coffee feel heavier or lighter in the mouth. Most people enjoy filter coffee that's at a strength of 1.3–1.4 per cent, and espresso coffee that is 8–10 per cent. This should put into perspective the relative strength of espresso compared to filter coffee.

A common misconception is that the strength of coffee refers to its caffeine content. However, two different varieties of coffee brewed to exactly the same strength (in total dissolved solids percentage) can have very different levels of caffeine.

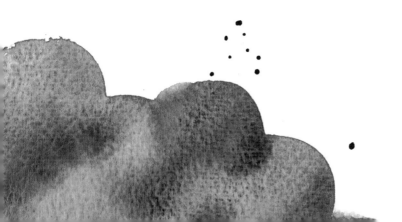

GRINDING & EQUIPMENT

No matter which method
you use to brew your coffee
at home, there are a few
pieces of equipment that will
make your life much easier.

Grinders

The way you grind your coffee will have a huge impact on the flavour and strength of your coffee brew. Grinding smashes the roasted coffee beans into tiny pieces, increasing the surface area exponentially. This increased surface area enables water to penetrate each particle, and dissolve or carry away things that make up the flavour of coffee.

Grind size & distribution

Grind size is very difficult to communicate because the equipment used to measure it isn't practical outside of a laboratory. In labs, technicians will use sieve sets, or laser diffractometers, to measure the number of particles of a certain size. In practice, we use the resulting strength of the brew to measure if we've started with the right grind size, and also the time it takes for the coffee to brew as an indication of whether the grind size is right. When we talk about grind sizes, we often refer to them under the assumption that all the ground particles are the exactly the same size, but of course this is unlikely, and usually not the case. Because the coffee is roasted and effectively dried to a moisture content of 1–2 per cent, it is extremely brittle, and therefore there can be a lot of very fine particles (called 'fines') created in the process.

In general, the grind size for brewing coffee varies a lot depending on the brewer it is destined for. Below I have outlined some examples of common things that you can relate the grind size to:

- A very fine powder like ground cinnamon. This would be a grind size suitable for Turkish brewing pots.

- Fine grains similar to fine table salt. This would be suitable for espresso.

- Medium-fine granules similar to white sugar, suitable for stovetop espresso.

- Medium-coarse granules similar to coarse sand, suitable for pour over.

- Coarse granules similar to very coarse sand, suitable for plunger.

Types of grinders

Historically coffee was ground by pounding the beans using a mortar and pestle, similar to the way spices are ground. Nowadays coffee is ground in three common ways.

Factory grinders
These are industrial-sized machines built to grind huge amounts of coffee per hour. Factories usually use several stages of grinding machines in a series, from large roller pre-breakers, to finer rollers, mixers and silos. Unless you're working in coffee production, you're unlikely to ever see machines like these.

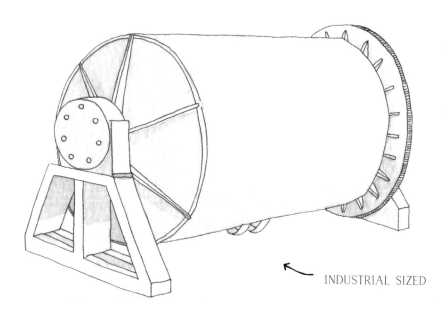

INDUSTRIAL SIZED

Electric burr grinders

These are the most common types of grinders used in cafés, shop roasters and as good domestic grinders. There are two types of burr grinders – flat burr and conical burr. The resulting difference between the two is not huge and not easily quantifiable. In general though, conical burr grinders are designed for espresso brewing and flat burr grinders for everything else. Conical burrs create a portion of very fine particles that slow down the rate of espresso extraction, allowing for a stronger brew. Conical burrs are generally used in domestic grinders because they can be produced more economically, in terms of cost and size – a conical burr has more cutting surface area than a flat burr of the same diameter. Flat burr grinders tend to produce less variance in particle size, allowing for a more even extraction with a longer brewing time, which is great for filter-coffee brewing or any method in which you can control the steep time.

Electric burr grinders can range in price from a few hundred dollars for a small domestic unit up to thousands for a commercial grinder. An electric burr grinder is highly recommended for simple, successful brewing at home, and there are many options that are of good quality and affordable.

FOUR BLADES SPIN,
SLICING UP THE BEANS

Electric "whirly-blade" grinders

Or spice grinders. While these are very commonly used for grinding coffee at home, they unfortunately don't do a very good job. The grinder chamber at the top of the grinder contains four blades which spin, slicing up the beans as they do so. There is very little control over the coffee particle size and the grinders tend to pulverise the coffee rather than creating evenly sized particles. The low price point makes them an attractive option, but as they grind coffee to a wide range of particle sizes, the coffee will brew with a large range of extractions, resulting in a lot more sour, acidic, bitter and harsh flavours.

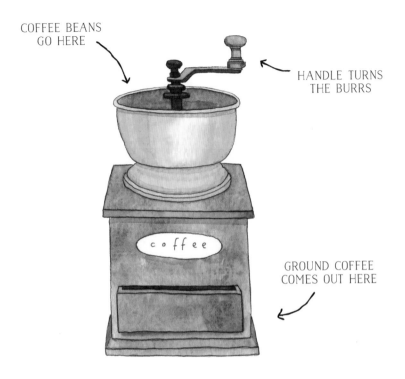

COFFEE BEANS
GO HERE

HANDLE TURNS
THE BURRS

GROUND COFFEE
COMES OUT HERE

coffee

Hand grinders

Hand grinders are simple and effective, with good examples making coffee that rivals expensive electric grinders. The only drawback is that it takes about a minute to grind enough coffee for one cup, compared with only a few seconds using an electric grinder. That said, they are perfect for the small kitchen, or for someone who travels a lot and loves to take coffee with them. Most hand grinders follow a similar design to that of a pepper mill – with a chamber in the top for whole beans, a middle grinding chamber with a fixed outer burr and rotating inner conical burr, and a lower chamber that holds the ground coffee. Look for one that is made from good materials, with steel or ceramic burrs.

Other equipment

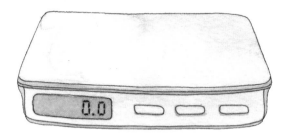

Scales Scales are great because they can help you quickly and accurately determine the amount of coffee and water you are using to brew with. For example, instead of having to decant a kettle of boiled water into a measuring pitcher, you can place the whole brewing apparatus on the scales, tare it off, and then add the correct amount of water required by weight. When weighing the coffee itself, scales are useful because of their accuracy especially when changing between different types of coffee, which can vary in density.

Timer

The length of time your coffee brews will greatly influence the flavour. In the same way that tea steeped for too long can ruin a cup, leaving coffee to brew for too long can ruin it. So, a timer for keeping track of the length of your brew is extremely useful. You don't need anything fancy, though.

Kettle

Some kettles are designed specifically for pouring water gently when brewing coffee, and while they're not absolutely necessary, they do look great in the kitchen. Whether you have a pouring kettle, or an electric kettle, just be sure to not let the water cool down too much after boiling and before brewing.

PRESSURED BREWING

Brewing coffee under pressure allows us to extract a higher strength coffee in a shorter amount of time. Espresso machines were developed in the early 1900s in Italy, so that numerous cups of coffee could be made quickly and to order. They were quite simple machines that used steam pressure to force hot water through a small amount of coffee. Initially this was done at quite high temperatures and relatively low pressure, but it was soon discovered that using water at a temperature of 90–95°C (194–203°F) yielded a far superior flavour. Brewing at higher pressures also resulted in a sweeter, stronger cup, and so spring-loaded piston pressurised machines quickly became the most popular.

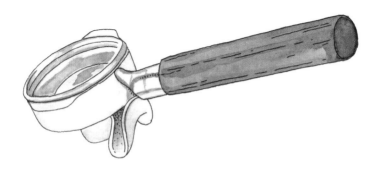

Stovetop percolator

The traditional stovetop coffee maker has not changed in design since the 1930s, when the popular Bialetti Moka Express was widely adopted. It is a very simple design – an octagonal aluminium water reservoir as the base, a small basket for holding ground coffee, and a chamber above to hold the brewed coffee. It's mechanism is extremely straightforward: the pot is placed on a stove, the water is heated, and as this happens the pressure inside the base of the pot increases to a point where it forces the water upwards through the bed of coffee. This pressure is less than that created by a modern espresso machine, or even the mechanical lever espresso machines of the 1920s, but it's enough to create a high temperature, and can extract more strength than is possible without pressure.

Equipment: Percolator and kettle.

Coffee: Your grind should be relatively fine, similar to the size of white sugar or table salt granules. Many people use a very fine grind, similar to espresso, or even finer, but I find that a coarser grind reduces the bitterness of the stovetop brew.

1. Bring 500 ml (17 fl oz) fresh water to the boil.

2. Rinse the percolator with hot water to warm it up and to ensure it's clean.

3. Fill the filter basket with coffee, ensuring the coffee bed is nice and even and flat, then brush any coffee from the edges of the basket.

4. Fill the base of the pot with boiled water, up to the height of the small pressure valve. If there is no valve, then fill to about three-quarters full. Place the filter basket into the base and firmly screw down the top.

5. Place the percolator on a stovetop (either gas or electric, induction will not work) over medium heat and open the lid. Because the water was hot to start with, the coffee will start flowing through the top of the stem quite quickly. Once coffee stops flowing from the stem, remove the pot from the heat, close the lid, and enjoy!

If you find your stovetop coffee is too weak, try using a finer grind size, or more coffee in the basket (and vice versa if it's too strong).

FILL THE BASKET
WITH COFFEE

FILL WITH BOILED WATER
TO HEIGHT OF PRESSURE VALVE

Espresso

By the 1920s, espresso machines contained electric heating elements, spring-loaded piston levers for pressure, and a steam boiler to heat and texture milk. There have been some developments in espresso machines since then, but surprisingly few. The largest development was the introduction of rotary pumps to produce the pressure required to make espresso, and more recently the introduction of fairly standard engineering equipment like the temperature controller PID. These developments have delivered some incremental improvements, but nothing revolutionary.

I think it's important to understand a bit about espresso machines and their intended purpose when considering them for use in your home. Some of the drawbacks are:

- they can take a long time to warm up
- using them successfully is largely driven by the quality of coffee grinder you have (so it needs to be good)
- it takes a fair bit of practice to make a good espresso at home
- they can take up a lot of space in your kitchen.

It's for these reasons that I don't have an espresso machine at home, and instead have a filter cone and a good grinder. If I wanted a stronger brew than filter coffee at home, I would probably choose a stovetop percolator over espresso. That said, a lot of people do have an espresso machine at home, and so here are a few tips to get the most out of them.

- **Use good quality coffee.** Starting with high quality coffee will give you the best start. Low quality coffee will never taste good, no matter how well it is brewed.

- **Make sure the espresso machine and grinder are well cleaned.** The biggest source of contamination in espresso coffee is dirty equipment. Be sure to clean the portafilter, basket, shower screen and group head very well before use.

- **Ensure the portafilter and espresso machine are thoroughly warmed up before use.** Running some hot water from the espresso machine through the empty portafilter can help warm it up more.

- **Always grind your coffee fresh and use an amount that is appropriate for the basket size.** As soon as coffee is ground, it starts to lose aromatics and flavour. Some machines will require a little more room between the top of the coffee bed and the top of the basket than other machines – so adjust accordingly. At the very least there should be 3–4 mm (⅛ in) of space from coffee bed to the top of the basket after the coffee is tamped down. In most cases this can be achieved by level-filling the basket before tamping.

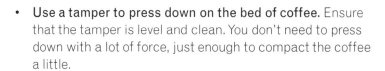

- **Use a tamper to press down on the bed of coffee.** Ensure that the tamper is level and clean. You don't need to press down with a lot of force, just enough to compact the coffee a little.

- **Aim to stop your shot at 30 seconds and/or when the shot weighs approximately twice the weight of the ground coffee used.** This is called the brew ratio, and it will dictate the strength and flavour of your espresso shot. For example, starting with 18 g ($\frac{5}{8}$ oz) of ground coffee, and using this to brew an espresso that weighs 36 g (1$\frac{1}{4}$ oz) is a brew ratio of 1:2. I would recommend staying within a brew ratio of 1:1.8 and 1:2.3 to get the best balance between flavour and strength. A higher ratio makes a stronger cup, but can result in sourness. A lower ratio will make a weaker cup, but it might have a better flavour. Play around with the ratio as every espresso machine is different.

- **Experiment with the brewing time by increasing or decreasing the grind size.** A finer grind will create more resistance for your espresso machine, and therefore the shot time will be longer. Conversely for a coarser grind. Generally espresso will only taste good if it is brewed between 25 and 35 seconds.

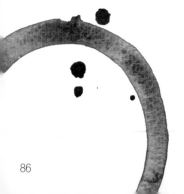

- **If making a coffee with milk, use high quality milk.**
  I recommend using whole milk, as fresh as you can get it, and one that has been through as little processing as possible. Look for certified organic and biodynamic milk, and, if you can, avoid milk that's been homogenised or high temperature treated.

NON-PRESSURISED BREWING

In this section we will be looking at brewing methods that do not use pressure in their brewing. They require less equipment, generally are easier to clean, and are easy to use at home.

Some of the most popular ones are:

- Plunger (or French press)

- Pour over
- Syphon

- AeroPress
- Chemex

ADD GROUND COFFEE
TO THE PLUNGER

ADD BOILED
WATER

BREW FOR
1 MINUTE

PUSH
PLUNGER
DOWN
&
ENJOY!

STIR & BREW
FOR 3 MINUTES

Plunger (French press)

The plunger is one of the simplest and oldest brew methods. Commonly made from a glass cylinder, with a metal stem and mesh filter, plungers come in a variety of sizes such as three-cup (350 ml/12 fl oz) or eight-cup (1 litre/34 fl oz). You will need to adjust your recipe to suit the plunger size, but for all filter coffee methods, 60 g (2⅛ oz) of coffee per 1 litre (34 fl oz) of water will yield a nice balance of strength and flavour.

Equipment: Plunger, kettle, scales and timer.

Coffee: Your grind should be quite coarse – it should feel like coarse sand between your fingers. For a three-cup plunger you'll need 21 g (¾ oz) of coffee and for an eight-cup you'll need 60 g (2⅛ oz).

1. Bring fresh water to the boil (500 ml/17 fl oz for three-cup or 1.25 litres/42 fl oz for eight-cup).

2. Rinse the plunger glass and filter with hot water to warm it up and to ensure it's clean. Drain.

3. Add the coffee to the plunger glass and fill with boiled water (350 ml/12 fl oz for three-cup, 1 litre/34 fl oz for eight-cup). Pour in the water quickly so it agitates the coffee a bit as you pour.

4. Start your timer and let the coffee brew for 1 minute, then give it a good stir. Brew for another 3 minutes.

5. Gently and slowly push the plunger down as far as it will go, so the plunger is holding the ground coffee firmly on the bottom of the plunger. Now pour and enjoy!

Pour over

Pour over can be made using a variety of different coffee makers, of different shapes and sizes. Popular brands include Melitta, Hario V60, Bee House and Clever Coffee Dripper, just to name a few. All of these brands work in essentially the same way: they are (or hold) a cone-shaped filter in which ground coffee is placed and then hot water is poured over to brew the coffee. The filter holds back the ground coffee solids, leaving a clear and light-bodied coffee brew to drip through into a cup. This is a very popular method for brewing at home, because it's simple and easy to clean up. Depending on the size of the maker, you can make between one and six cups at a time, but I normally recommend the two-cup size. The following instructions relate to the glass or ceramic drippers that use paper filters (some brands, such as the Clever Dripper don't require additional filters).

30 G (1 OZ) COFFEE
FOR 2 CUPS

PAPER FILTER SITS
IN THE CONE

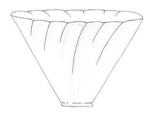

FILTER AND CONE SIT
IN THE HOLDER

Equipment: Coffee dripper/cone, filter paper, kettle, scales and timer.

Coffee: Your grind should be finer than what you would use for a plunger but coarser than espresso. A helpful measure of the proper grind size is the time it takes to brew, and 3 minutes is a good target. You'll need 30 g (1 oz) of coffee to make two cups.

1. Bring 1 litre (34 fl oz) fresh water to the boil.

2. Fit the filter paper into the cone and rinse the cone and your serving jug to warm them up and to ensure they're clean.

3. Place the coffee into the filter-lined cone and place the cone on top of your serving jug.

4. Place the jug and cone onto your scales. Pour in enough water to cover all the coffee, about twice the weight of the coffee (in this case about 60 g/2 oz of water). Start your timer for 3 minutes. Give the coffee and water a good stir, and leave to 'bloom' for about 30 seconds (this helps the coffee to degas and rearrange itself into an even bed, encouraging an even extraction).

5. Pour in more water, slowly and in a circular motion, about 150 g (5¼ oz) at a time, waiting about 20 seconds between pours, to bring the total amount of water to 500 g (1 lb 2 oz). Aim to finish pouring at the 2:15 minute mark, which will help get you to a total brew time of 3 minutes.

AeroPress

Compared with other brewing devices out there, the AeroPress is definitely the new kid on the block. The inventor Alan Adler of Stanford University (of Aerobie frisbee fame) developed the AeroPress with the aim to make a high quality single-cup brewer that could be brewed quickly. The result is sort of a hybrid between a plunger and a pour over, with a little amount of pressure used to force the brewed coffee through a paper filter. The AeroPress has gained a well-deserved reputation for producing consistently great coffee with minimal fuss.

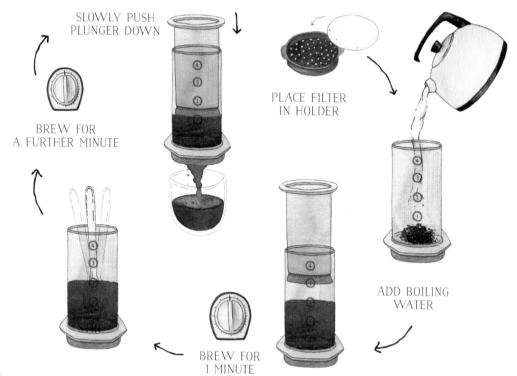

SLOWLY PUSH
PLUNGER DOWN

BREW FOR
A FURTHER MINUTE

PLACE FILTER
IN HOLDER

ADD BOILING
WATER

BREW FOR
1 MINUTE

The versatility of this brewer is highlighted by the huge number of different methods that are employed at the World AeroPress Championships (WAC) each year. We have found success with many of these methods from the WAC website, but our favourites are the simplest ones.

Equipment: AeroPress, filter paper, kettle, scales and timer.

Coffee: Your grind should be the same as you would use for pour over – finer than what you would use for a plunger but coarser than espresso. You'll need 15 g ($\frac{1}{2}$ oz) of coffee to make one cup.

1. Bring 500 ml (17 fl oz) fresh water to the boil.

2. Place the filter paper in the filter holder and attach it to the bottom of the AeroPress. Leave the plunger piece to one side for the moment. Place the bottom of the AeroPress on top of a cup and rinse with hot water. Allow to sit for a moment to warm the cup, then tip out the water and sit the cup and AeroPress on top of your scales.

3. Place the coffee into the AeroPress and fill with 300 g (10$\frac{1}{2}$ oz) of boiled water.

4. Carefully place the plunger part into the top of the AeroPress (this will stop the coffee dripping through the filter) and start your timer. After 1 minute, carefully remove the plunger and give the brew a good stir. Leave to brew for another 1 minute.

5. Gently and slowly push the plunger down until the coffee brew is completely pushed through the paper filter.

To clean the AeroPress, turn it so the filter holder is facing up, and remove the plastic filter holder. Slowly press the spent coffee and paper filter out into the bin or compost.

COFFEE DRINKS

Now you have the tools to make great coffee, here are some of the drinks you can make.

For filter coffee drinks, I recommend only brewing enough so you can drink it all straight away. Leaving coffee to sit on a hot plate (or even in a thermos), even for a short time, changes the flavour dramatically – some of the acids degrade into bitter and sour compounds. I also prefer to drink my filter coffee without milk, but if you prefer milk, try starting with just a little to taste. The following espresso-based recipes are all for brewing with a domestic machine.

Black espresso drinks

Espresso & short black
The espresso, or short black, is a small drink designed to be made and consumed quickly. It is the base of most espresso-brewed milk drinks, such as the cappuccino or latte.

To make

Freshly grind about 10 g (¼ oz) of coffee, or however much will fill the basket in your portafilter, leaving 3–4 mm (⅛ in) of space at the top when tamped. Brew for about 30 seconds to yield 20–25 g (¾–1 oz) of espresso. If it takes less than 30 seconds to yield that amount, make your grind size a little finer and try again. If you end up using more or less than 10 g (¼ oz) of coffee, aim for a ratio of 1:2 of ground coffee to brewed espresso.

It's good practice to first rinse your espresso cup with hot water, but be careful not to overheat the cup so you can still drink the espresso quickly.

25 G (1 OZ)
ESPRESSO

Double espresso / Long black / Americano

The double espresso, as it sounds, is basically two single-shot espressos, as per the recipe opposite.

The long black is from Australia and New Zealand, initially brewed by extracting the coffee with a ratio of 1:6 of ground coffee to resulting drink. More commonly now it is brewed by pulling a double espresso (with a ratio of 1:2) onto 50–100 ml (1¾–3½ fl oz) of hot water.

The Americano was so named by Italian baristas pulling very long espresso drinks for American tourists in Europe. It's essentially a very long long black, intended to mimic American filter coffee. Again, it's more commonly brewed now with a double espresso poured on top of 200 ml (7 fl oz) of hot water.

To make

For a double espresso freshly grind about 18 g (⅝ oz) of coffee or however much will fill the basket in your portafilter, leaving 3–4 mm (⅛ in) of space at the top when tamped. Brew for about 30 seconds to yield 35–45 g (1¼–1½ oz) of espresso. If it takes less than 30 seconds to yield that amount, make your grind size a little finer and try again. If you end up using more or less than 18 g (⅝ oz) coffee, aim for a ratio of 1:2 of ground coffee to brewed espresso.

For a long black or Americano, just pull a double espresso on top of your desired amount of hot water.

Milk espresso drinks

Espresso and hot milk is a great combination. Well-textured milk has a lovely silky mouthfeel and if it's good quality it should taste fresh and sweet, which complements the strong flavour of espresso coffee beautifully. If you like a milky coffee, or a weaker-flavoured coffee, I would recommend using just a single shot of espresso (or even less) in a 200 ml (7 fl oz) cup. If you prefer a strong coffee flavour then I would recommend starting with a double shot of espresso and adding milk to taste.

Small milk drinks

Macchiato

An espresso with a very small amount of milk added. Milk can be fresh or steamed.

Piccolo

Also known as a piccolo latte; an espresso with 20–30 ml (¾–1 fl oz) of steamed milk added.

Cortado

A Spanish-named drink; an espresso with about 100 ml (3½ fl oz) of steamed milk added.

Macchiato

] JUST A 'STAIN'
OF MILK

] 25 G (1 OZ)
ESPRESSO SHOT

Piccolo

20-30 ML
(³/₄-1 FL OZ) MILK [

25 G (1 OZ)
ESPRESSO SHOT [

Cortado

] 100 ML
(3½ FL OZ)
MILK

] 25 G (1 OZ)
ESPRESSO SHOT

Cappuccino

The cappuccino is the most famous milk-based coffee drink in the world. The name originated from the dark hazelnut-brown colour of espresso mixed with milk, which resembled the colour of the robes of Capuchin monks. The chocolate sprinkles are a recent addition to the cappuccino, and I consider them optional.

To make

Purge your steam wand and steam your milk to 60–65°C (140–150°F). To texture the milk, first use the tip of the steam wand to allow air in. Once the milk reaches 40°C (105°F), sink the steam wand deeper into the milk and continue to heat up to 60°C (140°F). Well-textured milk for a cappuccino should be glossy and free from large visible bubbles. It should look like lightly whipped meringue.

Brew an espresso into a 150 ml (5 fl oz) cup, and slowly pour the milk from a height of 5 cm (2 in). As the cup fills, lower the milk pitcher, and allow the lighter milk to skim out. This should make a rich cappuccino, with 1–2 cm (½–¾ in) of foamy milk on top.

FOAM IS 1–2 CM
(½–¾ IN) THICK

MILK SHOULD BE
THICK, GLOSSY AND
FREE OF BUBBLES
CHOCOLATE SPRINKLES
ARE OPTIONAL

150 ML
(5 FL OZ)
CUP

100 ML
(3½ FL OZ)
MILK

25 G (1 OZ)
ESPRESSO SHOT

Flat white

The flat white is a drink that's currently taking off in the US and the UK, but Australians and New Zealanders have been making them since the late 80s. Who developed the drink first is a subject of hot contention!

To make

Essentially the same as making a cappuccino, except the milk is textured much more thinly. Use the tip of the steam wand to add only a small amount of air into the milk, then sink the steam wand deeper into the milk and continue to heat up to 60°C (140°F). Well-textured milk for a flat white should be glossy and free from large visible bubbles. It should be quite thin, the consistency of pouring cream.

Brew an espresso into a 150 ml (5 fl oz) cup, and slowly pour the milk from a height of 5 cm (2 in). As the cup fills, lower the milk pitcher, and allow the lighter milk to skim out. This should make ½–1 cm (¼–½ in) of foamy milk on top.

THINLY TEXTURED MILK

100 ML
(3½ FL OZ)
MILK

25 G (1 OZ)
ESPRESSO SHOT

150 ML
(5 FL OZ)
CUP

Caffè latte

As the name just means 'coffee milk', there's no strict international definition for what a caffè latte is. In Europe, it can be stovetop-brewed coffee with hot milk, or it can be espresso and steamed milk. In Australia and New Zealand, the standard latte is an espresso in a 220 ml (7½ fl oz) glass, topped with textured milk. In the US and UK, lattes are usually larger – from 350–500 ml (12–17 fl oz).

To make

Again, essentially the same as making a cappuccino, except that the milk is textured to a medium level. Use the tip of the steam wand to add some air into the milk, then sink the steam wand deeper into the milk and continue to heat up to 60°C (140°F).Well-textured milk for a latte should be glossy and free from large visible bubbles.

Brew an espresso into a 220 ml glass, and slowly pour the milk from a height of 5 cm (2 in). As the cup fills, lower the pitcher, and allow the lighter milk to skim out. This should make 1–2 cm (½–¾ in) of foamy milk on top.

MILK IS THINNER THAN FOR A CAPPUCCINO, BUT THICKER THAN FOR A FLAT WHITE

220 ML
(7½ FL OZ)
MILK

25 G (1 OZ)
ESPRESSO SHOT

Cold coffee drinks

These can be very refreshing and are especially popular in places with hot summers. They can be made with espresso coffee, hot brewed filter coffee, or they can be brewed with cold water. In cafés, espresso-based iced coffees tend to be the best. Since the coffee is strong, you only have a small volume of hot liquid (about 40 ml/1¼ fl oz) to chill, so you can still brew it fresh and cool it quickly with the addition of ice and milk. With filter coffee, you have a much larger volume of hot liquid (about 230 ml/8 fl oz), which takes far more time to chill.

The difficulty associated with quickly chilling hot filter coffee means that cafés have been looking at alternative ways of brewing coffee for cold drinks. One widely adopted method is cold brew, which uses a very high proportion of coffee to water, and a very long steep time, sometimes 24 hours. This allows you to achieve the same strength of coffee brew as you would when using hot water. Cold water does not extract coffee in the same way as hot water does, so the flavour of cold brew coffee is normally very muted and a little bit chocolatey and malty. I would not recommend cold brew, and instead suggest using espresso or chilled filter coffee for cold coffee drinks.

Iced long black Three-quarters fill a glass with good quality ice and cold filtered water then top with a freshly brewed double espresso. You can adjust the strength by adjusting the amount of cold water you use – 150 ml (5 fl oz) is a good amount to start with.

Iced latte Three-quarters fill a glass with good quality ice and milk then top with a freshly brewed double espresso. If you like your coffee sweeter, add some raw sugar to the hot espresso before mixing it into the cold milk.

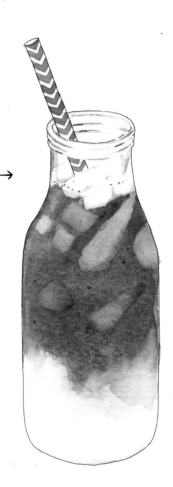

Iced filter coffee Follow the recipe for a regular filter coffee on page 93, but using coffee that's extremely finely ground, almost to a powder. Once the coffee is brewed, pour into a glass filled with ice and stir until the ice is melted and the coffee is cold. Add a few fresh ice cubes to keep the coffee cold. The finely ground coffee will make the brew much stronger than usual, but the diluting ice will balance the strength.

Coffee spritz

Three-quarters fill a glass with good quality ice and tonic water then top with a freshly brewed double espresso. It sounds like an odd combination, but the quinine in the tonic works really well with the body of the espresso, and makes for a very refreshing drink.

50 G (2 OZ)
ESPRESSO SHOT

FILL WITH
TONIC WATER

INDEX

A

AeroPress 94
Americano 99
arabica vs. robusta 10

B

batch size and airflow (roasting) 30
black espresso drinks 98
Brazil 56
brewing methods
  AeroPress 94
  espresso machine 84
  pour over 92
  plunger (French press) 90
  stovetop percolator 82
browning 34

C

caffè latte 104
cappuccino 102
certifications 47
  certified organic 47
  fair trade 48
  Cup of Excellence 49
certified organic 47
child labour 43
coffee pods 53
coffee spritz 107

cold coffee drinks 105
Colombia 58
cortado 100
cultivation 12
Cup of Excellence 49

D

double espresso 99
drinks 97
  Americano 99
  caffè latte 104
  cappuccino 102
  coffee spritz 107
  cortado 100
  double espresso 99
  espresso 98
  flat white 103
  iced filter coffee 106
  iced latte 106
  iced long black 106
  latte 104
  long black 99
  macchiato 100
  piccolo 100
  short black 98
drying 23
  mechanical drying 25
  passive drying 23

E

economic differences 16
electric 'whirly-blade' grinders 76
electric burr grinders 75
environmental concerns 42
espresso 98
espresso machines 84
Ethiopia 57
extraction & brewing 68
extraction & strength 69

F

factory grinders 74
fair trade 48
final temperature (roasting) 31
first crack 32
flat white 103
flavour 51
French press 90
freshness 36

G

grind size and distribution 72
grinders 74
  electric burr grinders
  electric 'whirly blade' grinders 76
  factory grinders 74
  hand grinders 77
  spice grinders 76
grinding & equipment 72
growing regions 15
Guatemala 59

H

hand grinders 77
harvest information 45
history 10
history 12

I

iced filter coffee 106
iced latte 106
iced long black 106
Indonesia 61
instant coffee 52

K

Kenya 62
kettle 79

L

latte 104
long black 99
lot separation 20

M

macchiato 100
making informed choices 42
mechanical drying 25
milk 65
milk espresso drinks 100

N

natural processing 21
non-pressurised brewing 89

P

passive drying 23
percolator 82
perfect roast 34
piccolo 100
picking 20
plunger 90
pour over 92
pressured brewing 81
processing 21
  natural 21
  pulped natural 22
  washed 22
production 16
pulped natural 22

R

regional characteristics 55
  Brazil 56
  Colombia 59
  Ethiopia 57
  Guatemala 59
  Indonesia 61
  Kenya 62
  Rwanda 60
ripeness and quality 18
roast date 45
roasting 27
  batch size 30
  browning 34
  cooling 31
  flavour 30
  machines 27
  process 29

temperature 31
time 30
stages 32
roasting for flavour 30
roasting machines 27
roasting process 28
roasting time 30
Rwanda 60

S

scales 78
selecting coffee 40
short black 98
spice grinders 76
stages of roasting 32
steaming milk 66
stovetop percolator 82
strength 51

T

temperature profile (roasting) 31
texturising milk 66
timer 79
traceability 40
type of roast 50
types of coffee 52

V

varieties 10

W

washed processing 22
water 63
what to look for on the bag 44
whole bean or ground? 54

ABOUT THE AUTHOR

Jason Scheltus trained in coffee roasting at Monmouth Coffee, London for two years, then returned to his home town of Melbourne to co-found Market Lane Coffee, a specialty coffee company with five retail locations and over 50 staff. He works as a coffee buyer and in quality control for coffee roasting, drink preparation and service. He has been a judge in Cup of Excellence, national barista competitions, and AeroPress brewing competitions.

Published in 2016 by Smith Street Books
Melbourne | Australia
smithstreetbooks.com

ISBN: 978-1-925418-14-9

CIP data is available from the National Library of Australia

Publisher: Paul McNally
Senior editor: Hannah Koelmeyer, Tusk studio
Illustration, design & layout: Daniella Germain

Printed & bound in China by C&C Offset Printing Co., Ltd.

Book 16
10 9 8 7 6 5 4 3 2 1